This book belongs to:

_____

A catalogue record for this book is available from the British Library

Published by Ladybird Books Ltd
A Penguin Company
Penguin Books Ltd, 80 Strand, London WC2R 0RL, UK
Penguin Books Australia Ltd, Camberwell, Victoria, Australia
Penguin Group (NZ) Ltd, 67 Apollo Drive, Rosedale, North Shore 0632, New Zealand

13
© LADYBIRD BOOKS LTD MCMXCVIII. This edition MMVI

ISBN-13: 978-1-84646-070-8

Printed in China

The Ugly Duckling

illustrated by Gilly Marklew

The eggs

Mother Duck

4

The Ugly Duckling

The ducklings

Once upon a time
there were seven eggs.

Six ducklings were beautiful.

One duckling was not.

"You are ugly," said
Mother Duck.

"Go away."

The Ugly Duckling
met a cow.

"You are ugly,"
said the cow.

"Go away."

The Ugly Duckling
met a cat.

"You are ugly,"
said the cat.

"Go away."

The Ugly Duckling
met a rabbit.

"You are ugly,"
said the rabbit.

"Go away."

17

The Ugly Duckling
met a boy.

"You are ugly,"
said the boy.

"Go away."

The Ugly Duckling
met a girl.

"You are ugly,"
said the girl.

"Go away."

The Ugly Duckling
was all alone.

He was very sad.

One day, the Ugly Duckling saw some beautiful swans.

"Look in the water," said the swans.

"You are beautiful,"
said the swans.

"Come with us."

And he did.

Read It Yourself is a series of graded readers designed to give young children a confident and successful start to reading.

Level 1 is suitable for children who are making their first attempts at reading. The stories are told in a very simple way using a small number of frequently repeated words. The sentences on each page are closely supported by pictures to help with reading, and to offer lively details to talk about.

About this book

The pictures in this book are designed to encourage children to talk about the story and predict what might happen next.

The opening page shows a detailed scene which introduces the main characters and vocabulary appearing in the story.

After a discussion of the pictures, children can listen to an adult read the story or attempt to read it themselves. Unknown words can be worked out by looking at the beginning letter *(what sound does this letter make?)*, and deciding which word would make sense.

Beginner readers need plenty of encouragement.